New Boots for Quack

Written by Michèle Dufresne • Illustrated by Tracy La Rue Hohn

PIONEER VALLEY EDUCATIONAL PRESS, INC.

Dad can see blue boots.

I can see orange boots.

Dad can see black boots.

I can see yellow boots.

Dad can see pink boots.

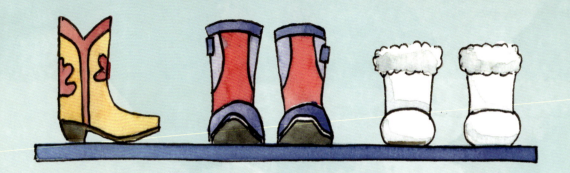

I can see white boots.

Dad can see green boots.

I can see red boots.